First Steps to

TAROT

Elizabeth Wheldrake

AXIOM

With love and gratitude to my family, friends and clients.

ISBN: 1 86476 027 3

Axiom
Australia

Welcome
the journey

Contents
page

The Tarot

offers thoughts and inspiration

on all aspects of life.

What is Tarot?

The modern cards consist of two sections: the major arcana and the minor arcana. The word *arcana* is well suited to the Tarot, as it means mystery.

The mysterious and mystical sources of the Tarot are attributed by some to such diverse cultures as ancient Egyptian, pagan Celtic and the Cabbalists. The British Museum has many decks dating back to the 1470s from Italy and later from France. The common feature of the Tarot, regardless of time or place, is that decks of any significance describe *the state of the world*. Brother John of Brefeld, a Swiss monk, used this term to describe cards similar to the Tarot in 1377. He thought the cards were used to teach the upper classes rules for their privileged status, whilst training the lower classes to serve their masters faithfully. Gambling games and fortune telling have also been associated with the Tarot over the centuries. Not surprisingly, these were denounced at various times by church or state.

A Challenge For The 21st Century
The Tarot continues to speak directly to each generation by responding to the needs of its individuals.

The Tarot promotes quiet examination of the alternatives available for responsible decision making.

The Tarot guides towards a more spiritual and less materialistic life.

In other words, *The Tarot helps each individual grow with integrity towards a more authentic self*.

The cards therefore, should be used with some dignity and in moderation.

Single cards
These indicate a method of approach, a stage of life or a person with particular characteristics. Each card should be seen as gender inclusive.

Spreads
Traditional spreads may be found in any Tarot publication. The Celtic cross given towards the end of this book, is one such layout. The pyramid, on the other hand, is my own response which provides a spread, with sufficient depth and breadth for the modern client.

The Major Arcana
Twenty one cards are arranged in three groups of seven. These groups represent increasingly difficult issues which challenge our integrity as we progress through life. The twenty second card connects the whole into the ongoing cycle of growth and reintegration. This naturally continues to death and ultimately, rebirth.

The Minor Arcana
The 56 Cards appear in four suits, as with standard playing cards. In addition there is an extra court card in each suit.

The Suits		
Cups	=	Relationships (Water)
Wands	=	Energy (Fire)
Swords	=	Intelligence (Air)
Pentacles	=	Income (Earth)

The suits focus on people, personalities and their responses to age old situations. The cards are gender inclusive. Note: It is the *characteristics* which are important, rather than the gender.

The Fool 0

The sun shines as the traveller sets out cheerfully at the start of this new and important journey. Meanwhile the little dog offers the voice of caution.

Interpretation

Start this fresh chapter of life with optimism. Use the knowledge and experiences from the past to make this a positive period.

The Magician 1

Resting on the table are the cups, pentacles, swords and wands. The magician is poised to work with them under the sign of infinity.

Interpretation

All these personal resources are here to be used now. Keep a healthy, balanced and positive approach in this new era.

The High Priestess 2

A religious young woman sits in quiet contemplation with the book of knowledge in her lap. The new moon brings fertile thoughts and the tapestry provides a rich harvest.

Interpretation

Plan the new goals with calm confidence. Allow for flexibility and expect some promising outcomes.

THE HIGH PRIESTESS

The Empress 3

The earth mother sits centre stage in this fertile setting of corn, forest and waterfall. Her crown glistens with the twelve stars of the zodiac.

Interpretation

The focus is on a nurturing, nesting period. It is important though, to retain the vital sense of personal identity at this time.

THE EMPRESS.

The Emperor 4

This venerable ruler sits firmly on the throne. The orb, sceptre and rams declare his power. This figure may be younger or older and either male or female. The common feature is of taking control and making important decisions.

Interpretation

A strong father figure will protect and support in times of need. A natural authoritarian, he or she prefers to give the orders.

The Hierophant 5

The High Priest, sometimes known as the Pope, blesses his bishops in a formal ceremony. The cross and keys of Rome add to the traditional symbols of Christianity.

Interpretation

Official blessings are given and well deserved. On-going care and confirmation will nurture growth and development for the enterprise.

THE LOVERS.

The Lovers 6
The archangel hovers overhead in the Garden of Eden. A mountain retreat is available, but the serpent is about to eat the forbidden fruit.

Interpretation
This complex and tempting personal dilemma requires careful consideration. Listen to and act on the inner voice of reason.

The Chariot 7
The chariot moves forward smoothly, pulled by the well harnessed mythical creatures. Images of balance, guidance and success complete the scene.

Interpretation
Welcome this progressive phase. Much ground can now be covered, self-control and inner harmony will be maintained.

THE CHARIOT.

Pause now. The next group of cards will become progressively more challenging.

Strength 8

Under the halo of infinity, a woman handles the lion like a favourite pet. The well developed spiritual direction, shows in the mountain peak. The whole picture is infused with light.

Interpretation

Courage overcomes the anger which holds back personal growth. The inner strength gained is a very real victory.

The Hermit 9

Father Time looks for illumination to the star lit lamp. He stands alone on the mountain top, the classical place of meditation.

Interpretation

Time is precious. Clear out deep seated burdens from the past, as they seriously limit the present. Only then, is it possible for the real self to emerge. Reincarnation too, depends on what use is made of the present. Therefore, it is doubly important to attend to this challenge.

The Wheel of Fortune 10
Classical symbols support a seemingly endless rotation of life. The good ascends with Anubis, and is counteracted by the bad descending with Typhon. However the symbols from the Book of Revelations and the Sphinx hold the key to the answer.

Interpretation
There is an orderly pattern. By rising above material things in the next upswing, life will be far richer.

Justice 11
Justice will be done. The symbols are clear. Although the scales are balanced, the sword of Damocles is poised to fall either way.

Interpretation
Be fair and compassionate in all circumstances in order to receive true justice. A generous and forgiving approach is needed.

The Hanged Man 12
The saintly halo features in this stylised, yoga-like position. Twelve leaves on the branch in earlier decks represent both the Apostles and the signs of the zodiac.

Interpretation
Be objective and logical about future plans. Sacrifices will be required in order to achieve significant, long term goals. The results will justify the commitment.

Death 13
The difficult path leads to a sun-lit horizon. Blessings are given for both the end and the beginning.

Interpretation
Welcome the promising new beginning. Leave the past gently but firmly behind and go forward joyfully.

TEMPERANCE.

Temperance 14

A pool of water is murky and the liquid flows only between the cups. The path is long and difficult. It leads however to the light on the mountain, confirmed by the symbols of archangels and the Tarot.

Interpretation

Things appear to be quite stagnant. With patience, new promising personal goals will soon appear on the horizon.

Pause again. The remaining seven cards will provide the ultimate challenges which continue to face the human race.

The Devil 15

Here is the blackest picture, of a couple chained in hell. The devil dominates, along with other symbols of his power.

Interpretation

The hell may be inherited or personally made. Kindness to oneself is vital. The courage to forgive can then dissolve the darkest thoughts and heal the soul.

THE DEVIL .

The Tower 16
A bolt of lightning strikes. The seemingly impregnable tower quakes and shatters from its foundations. Not even the rulers of the world escape the crash.

Interpretation
A false exterior protects or hides the truth. Now, shattering events seem likely. Time is the healer. The new foundation will then be stronger, firmer and more authentic.

The Star 17
Spilt water flows all around. However, the bright morning star in its galaxy, dominates the scene.

Interpretation
When everything seems to have been lost, the guiding star appears. It points to recovery, followed by the renewal of faith, for a brighter future.

The Moon 18

The old notion of excess and madness at the time of the full moon is evident. The path is very slippery and the water badly disturbed.

Interpretation

Life has its darker side, with excess and unstable people or situations. Help may be needed to understand and accept this difficult time.

THE MOON.

The Sun 19

The sun shines brightly and wisely on the earth. The child appears on a white horse, carrying the banner of victory.

Interpretation

True happiness is fully appreciated as it has been well earned. The real pleasures and joys of living are warmly shared.

THE SUN .

Judgment 20

The dead rise up from their coffins as an angel sounds the final judgement call. The scene, reminiscent of Revelations, the last book of The Bible is very clear.

Interpretation

Ultimately we are responsible and answerable for ourselves. It is time to be prepared to account for all the decisions of the past and receive what is due.

The World 21

The four living creatures of Revelations are shown in the four corners of the world. So too are the classical symbols of the Sphinx. The veil is worn lightly by the woman as she dances in the wreath of victory.

Interpretation

Having conquered fears and doubts, learned and done so much, it is time to celebrate. The priceless treasure of integrity is gained and the world opens up fresh vistas.

And so... on to The Fool and with new eyes start the next, even more promising section of this journey, we call Life.

The *Suit* Of Cups

The cups are associated primarily with feelings and relationships. They are also related to physical, emotional and spiritual health.

- Water is the chief element.
- The main focus is on the need to establish and maintain healthy relationships, based on mutual respect and friendship.
- The characters show people with these traits or these situations:

Ace of Cups
An aura surrounds the hand which holds the cup. Watery elements and symbols dominate the scene, whilst the dove and cross provide a peaceful blessing.

ACE & CUPS.

Interpretation
There is enormous potential for a very healthy relationship. With care and consideration this could develop into something deeper and more significant.

2 Cups

The angel's wings hover above the Egyptian symbol of earth, fire, air and water. A traditional love-nest complements the scene in which the couple salute each other.

Interpretation

These two people are well matched to further explore their goals and values. The focus is on the development of the harmony and trust already evident.

3 Cups

Dressed for a special event, the women are offering a toast. A wonderful harvest is all around.

Interpretation

A joyful event will be welcome. An engagement, commitment, marriage, birth, birthday or special occasion is shown.

4 Cups

Arms folded, the person sits alone looking pensively down. The cup and what it offers go unnoticed.

Interpretation

Relationship issues are less than satisfactory or non existent. A significant effort is required to improve the situation.

5 Cups

The figure looks at the overturned cups and at the strong ripples on the water. The two upright cups are out of the line of vision.

Interpretation

There is a tendency to dwell in the past. It is time to move on to welcome the new opportunities which are very close.

6 Cups

The older person looks back a little pensively. The younger one willingly carries the flower filled cup to a new destination.

Interpretation

The old ways are now left behind and the next cycle is beginning. This may involve a change of attitude and new direction. There may be an accompanying change of location.

7 Cups

This figure reaches towards the cups, each of which contain something different. The cups themselves are resting in the clouds.

Interpretation

Dreams present a variety of ideas. They should not be allowed to slip away, as sometimes happens. It is very important to develop definite plans to fulfil the dreams.

8 Cups

The figure walks the difficult path with the help of a staff. Despite the dark rocks, clear waters are ahead. There is a focus on the changing phase of the moon and the upright cups.

Interpretation

At last the emotional upheavals of the past are left behind. Calm times lie ahead, both personally and in relationships.

9 Cups

These cups are grouped like trophies. A cheerful figure is seated in front with arms folded to form the sign of infinity.

Interpretation

Relationship issues are resolved and personal growth achieved. Happiness won through personal efforts can now be maintained.

10 Cups

The couple embrace each other and their children. The placid waters flow gently by. Overhead glows the rainbow.

Interpretation

An ongoing commitment to a healthy relationship is shown. Spiritual guidance is assured and contentment earned.

Page of Cups

Gentle waves set the watery scene. The young person looks quietly at the cup containing a fish.

Interpretation

A gentle awakening to the possibility of a new romantic relationship. This may be for the first time. Alternatively, it may suggest a readiness for such a situation.

PAGE of CUPS.

Knight of Cups

The dazzling knight on a fine horse gallantly offers the cup in a romantic gesture. The beautiful location complements the scene.

Interpretation

A romantic offer or the romantic stage in a relationship. All the traditional features of this stage are implied. eg. flowers, wine and idyllic situations.

Queen of Cups

Her fragile position is close to swirling water where she sits pensively looking at the ciborium. Mermaids and fish add to the watery scene.

Interpretation

Someone who is deep emotionally and often intuitive. She may have been a victim in the past and now chooses to remain one. It is preferable though, to make positive changes.

King of Cups

The ruler is surrounded by symbols of the sea. However he sits well above the water with the fish leaping around. The ship too is quite safe.

Interpretation

Healing, health and all related professions are in focus. This potential could be developed. The person should give more attention to his or her own needs which may be neglected.

The Suit Of Wands

- The wands are associated with energy, courage and the love of life.

- Fire is the chief element.

- The main focus is on living life to the full, meeting obstacles with courage and knowing when to stop.

Ace of Wands

An aura surrounds the hand which holds the wand aloft, like an Olympic torch. Clear water and a large castle provide the setting.

Interpretation

This new project has enormous potential. An energy filled time, which should be used to good effect. Stay balanced as the ideas and action gain momentum.

2 of Wands

The globe rests firmly in the hand as the character looks out confidently. He sees fresh vistas of mountains, lake and a fertile landscape.

Interpretation

There may have been slight delay but everything is now moving forward. Exciting plans can be made for future expansion. These may be quite large scale and include travel.

3 of Wands

A golden light shines on the entire scene. The traveller surveys the broad horizons from his vantage point.

Interpretation

A most expansive period in which much can be achieved. A wonderful action packed time which often includes long distance travel.

4 of Wands

Two people share the fruits of their harvest. They are standing under a canopy decorated with symbols of triumph. The bridge in the background leads to a castle in the air.

Interpretation

The honesty, effort and shared commitment to a team or partnership pays dividends. It brings a well-earned reward for both the personal and or professional relationship.

5 of Wands

The people involved appear active, enthusiastic and confident. There is clearly something of a challenge involved.

Interpretation

Individual and team efforts must be harmonious and focused on the goal. Less than enthusiastic players may need a different environment.

6 of Wands

The crown and wreath are held high in triumph as the victor leads the honours parade.

Interpretation

Inner battles have been won and self congratulations due. Wonderful progress can now be made.

7 of Wands

A well prepared mountaineer strides out. The day is clear and fine.

Interpretation

This character needs action and must avoid stagnation. A fresh challenge should be found and interesting plans formulated if one is not on offer.

Suggests adventure lies ahead.

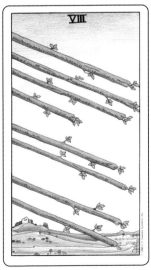

8 of Wands

The long stretch of water and clear skies provide the setting. The wands are thrown forward, javelin like, towards the target.

Interpretation

The previous delays are over. Take advantage of this fine stretch of plain sailing for all plans. These may well include romance.

9 of Wands

The wands form a barrier behind the character who appears to be under some stress. The original green fields seem very far away.

Interpretation

Things have not gone according to plan and the person is now trapped. It is necessary to fully acknowledge the difficult situation and seek new insights and approaches.

10 of Wands

The story-book village is in sight. Staggering towards it is the traveller who is weighed down badly by the wands.

Interpretation

The burden should be shed. Delegate if possible. If not a superhuman effort will be required to complete the task. Rest and recuperation will then restore the body and the spirit.

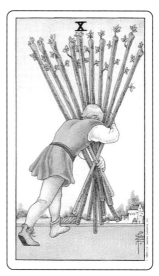

Page of Wands

The young person pauses on his journey. He looks ahead to a welcoming landscape.

Interpretation

There is a message of good news which may have been awaited. It is now possible to proceed with longer term plans.

Knight of Wands

This adventuresome knight is slightly out of control. The horse also bucks and rears.

Interpretation

A light-hearted person is in focus who may not take life seriously. Otherwise a light-hearted approach or leisure activity is needed if someone is overworked.

Queen of Wands

The queen sits easily on her throne in a position of authority and balance. She has selected a flower along with the wand as her symbols of office. The cat adds a magical touch.

Interpretation

A natural leader, she leads by her positive example. Lively, yet grounded, she enjoys all aspects of her well-balanced life.

King of Wands

The king is a splendid, colourful figure, with rich red robes, wand and hair. He looks out with confidence to view the world. A salamander, the symbol of fire is by the throne.

Interpretation

A bold person who vigorously embraces life. He enthuses everyone with his big, imaginative plans.

The Suit Of Swords

The swords are associated with the use of intelligence in thought, word and deed.

Air is the chief element.

The main focus is on expansion of the mind, balanced thinking and humane decision making.

The characters show people with these traits or these situations:

ACE of SWORDS.

Ace of Swords

An aura surrounds the strong hand which holds the sword firmly in the air. Threaded into the crown is an olive branch and palm leaf.

Interpretation

A challenging new idea with great and humane potential. Resistance to the plan may have to be approached with care and consideration.

2 of Swords

The blindfolded figure sits with crossed swords. The water is very disturbed and the new moon significant.

Interpretation

Some pressure needs to be resisted in this difficult situation. Wait until all the information is available and make a very clear assessment before arriving at a firm decision.

3 of Swords

Storm clouds fill the entire picture and the three swords pierce the heart very deeply.

Interpretation

It may be necessary to fully acknowledge a broken heart. Grief is appropriate in its season. There comes a moment when the first steps to recovery should be taken for healing to occur.

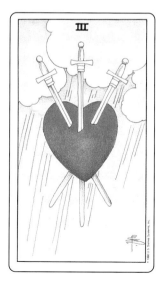

4 of Swords

The effigy on the tombstone is in the traditional pose of prayer. Three of the swords hang like a banner in the church. A stained glass window completes the scene.

Interpretation

Quiet thought or prayer is needed to cope with the daily demands of life. Here is a definite on-going responsibility to look after oneself, properly and regularly.

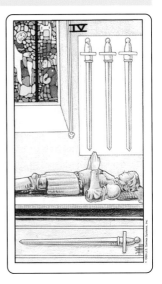

5 of Swords

Those who lost the fight look towards the threatening clouds and rough sea. So too does the apparent winner.

Interpretation

A compromise position might be in the best interests of all concerned. This could be difficult to accept but may well be the only viable option.

6 of Swords

The swords are at rest. The people are propelled away from the heavily rippled waters and into clear seas.

Interpretation

A calm period is ahead where problems can be put aside. It is up to the individual concerned to be positive and resist the self-inflicted headaches of the past.

7 of Swords

The person looks back to check that his deceit has not been observed. He is fleeing quickly and stealthily with the swords, which are here seen as stolen goods.

Interpretation

Tact, diplomacy and caution should be used in order to achieve the desired results. Watch for a little deceit and take sensible everyday precautions.

8 of Swords

The captive is backed against a wall of swords with small pools in the foreground. The castle and clear water appear in the distance.

Interpretation

The original situation may not be of the person's making. The current conditions though are mainly self-imposed and can be changed at any time.

9 of Swords

The black setting and the figure bolt upright in bed indicate a nightmare. The swords however point to the east and the zodiac symbols decorate the bed cover.

Interpretation

There is hope out of this darkness. A period of respite is vital, in order to recover from the dismal and depressing situation.

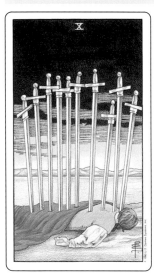

10 Swords
Stabbed deeply and repeatedly in the back, the person appears to be dead. Nevertheless, the new dawn is clearly featured.

Interpretation
It is time to acknowledge the nightmare from the past. Only then is it possible to move on fully and welcome the new future.

Page of Swords
A young person stands on slightly higher ground with a backdrop of mountains. He waves the sword in a testing sort of attitude. Light storm clouds are starting to gather.

Interpretation
Someone may try to wound with a few hurtful words. These comments may give food for thought, but more likely should simply be ignored.

PAGE of SWORDS.

Knight of Swords

He speeds in brandishing his sword with some agitation. The thunderous clouds add to the atmosphere.

Interpretation

Carefully chosen words are required. These will clear the air of a situation which might have been festering for some time.

KNIGHT of SWORDS .

QUEEN of SWORDS.

Queen of Swords

Seated above the cloud line, the queen extends one hand beyond the sword. A cherub, butterfly and moon are used symbolically to decorate the throne.

Interpretation

Cool and withdrawn, this person seeks solitude. It is possible though that she needs to trust again, and be open to the potential of new relationships.

King of Swords

He sits in control on a high throne. His sword is held for good effect in the spartan landscape. Waxing and waning moons add to the scene.

Interpretation

A person of definite opinions speaks clearly and influentially. While useful in certain circumstances, a more humane approach may sometimes be preferred.

KING of SWORDS.

The Suit Of Pentacles

The pentacles are associated with the provision of income, basic needs and contentment.

Earth is the chief element.

The main focus is on creating a lifestyle in which simple pleasures and an adequate income combine to provide real satisfaction.

The characters are shown as people with these traits or these situations:

Ace of Pentacles

An aura surrounds the hand which carefully holds the pentacle. The setting is one of fertile fields and flowers. A hedged archway leads to the mountaintop behind.

Interpretation

A money-making opportunity is presented. This should be carefully considered from all angles before proceeding further.

2 of Pentacles

In this balancing act the two pentacles fit neatly into the sign of infinity. Meanwhile the ships are cresting the biggest waves with ease.

Interpretation

Life is getting back into balance both generally and financially. This makes for optimism and forward movement for major plans.

3 of Pentacles

The stonemason's quality work is being completed in the crypt. Looking on with admiration are his masters.

Interpretation

A determined approach has earned a career highlight. The accompanying acknowledgment is well deserved. It provides the incentive to pursue new goals.

4 of Pentacles

Modern skyscrapers provide the setting. This one dimensional person holds very tightly on to the pentacle and looks straight ahead.

Interpretation

There is a meanness of spirit and perhaps a preoccupation with money. A change of attitude is needed in order to see a different, more personally satisfying approach.

5 of Pentacles

These destitute people are stumbling in the blizzard. The pentacles shine in the stained glass window.

Interpretation

There is a need to be thankful for the simple things. They are often taken for granted and not always properly acknowledged in our somewhat material world.

6 of Pentacles

The scales of justice are clearly balanced as the merchant gives out money to the poor.

Interpretation

This person knows that something more valuable than money makes life truly worthwhile. The goodness of kind deeds brings its own reward.

7 of Pentacles

The figure looks unhappily down onto the drab scene of the accumulated pentacles. However the single pentacle, close to the brightly coloured boot, is also in the picture.

Interpretation

There is a desire to change direction. There may be more to life than the current, somewhat jaded situation. The situation may need a little more consideration.

8 of Pentacles

Working productively in a natural setting, is a very skilled, creative person. The tree is used to display the quality of his work. A peaceful village provides the idyllic background.

Interpretation

A special talent should be used to develop in a new and personally satisfying direction. This may involve some long term change, with renewed pleasure and profit in work.

9 of Pentacles

An elegant young woman stands with confidence in the garden, where the pentacles and the fruits share equal place.

Interpretation

The person has found balance and harmony. A sound understanding of money is complemented by inner wisdom and a life in tune with nature.

10 Pentacles

The three generations are connected by the harvest and the home. They sit together under the archway. Both the scales and the placement of the pentacles are clearly balanced.

Interpretation

Secure in all ways, these people understand the true meaning of abundance. Their wisdom and contentment is well earned.

Page of Pentacles

The young person holds a single pentacle with care. He stands lightly and at ease in the fertile valley. The grass, trees and mountains add to the scene.

Interpretation

A little money and talent may be well used and lead to other opportunities. For example, a leisure activity might develop eventually into a career.

Knight of Pentacles

A young man sits easily on a dark, placid work horse. He holds the pentacle comfortably. His gaze takes in the rich cultivated land and newly ploughed fields.

Interpretation

Income is assured for this practical person. Furthermore, it will suit the needs and personality of the character concerned.

Queen of Pentacles

A mature woman holds the pentacle lightly. All around her are scenes of the rich earth, mountain peaks and other symbols of nature.

Interpretation

Balanced and sensual, this person understands money and values the gifts of the earth.
She gives out and receives accordingly.

King of Pentacles

He dominates the scene on his large throne. The pentacle is shown as his symbol of office. Castles in the air feature quite largely in the background.

Interpretation

Suggests a keen interest and success in career and making money. He cares for others financially too.

Alpha and Omega

And so we come to the end. But the end is much more like the beginning.

There is so much more to the Tarot, that once started, opens up endless fascinating insights and avenues for thought.

Travel, perhaps to London and The British Museum, to see a host of Tarot decks dating from the later part of the fifteenth century.

Go to Rochester, on the Pilgrims Way to Canterbury. There on the wall of a Christian cathedral you will see part of a thirteenth century oil painting of The Wheel Of Fortune.

Pursue the algebra of the ancient world of the sphinx, entwined with the Hebrew Kabbalah. Study the connections with astrology and numerology.

Translate the Egyptian hieroglyphs.

Explore the relationship between the Apocrypha of the Old Testament and the Apocalypse or Revelations of the New Testament.

Revisit the concepts of reintegration and rebirth.

Reflect on the cards or use Tarot affirmations. Have a reading, from someone reputable.

- The Tarot cards still accurately describe the state of our world. Now as always, they are a guide to our society. They give hope in the most difficult times and lead to the path of integrity.

- The gentle sounding word Karma means action. Each action has a direct consequence.

- Any of these steps will lead you to take greater responsibility for your own actions.

Be strong
true to the self
as well as others

Six Month Spread

The Client / Enquirer
**Shuffles the cards well and cuts them once or
twice in the traditional manner.**

The Reader
1. Set out the top 15 cards in a pyramid, starting
at the lower left hand corner, with 5 cards at the
base.

2. Read from 1 through to 15, taking 3 cards
per month, for the first 3 months and 2 cards
per month thereafter.

Example
Card 1. 2 of Wands
There may have been slight delay, but
everything is in forward motion now. Exciting plans can now be
made for future expansion. These may be large scale and include
travel.

Card 2. King of Wands
A bold person, vigorously embraces life, who enthuses everyone
with his big imaginative plans.

Card 3. 7 of Swords
Tact, diplomacy and caution should be used in order to achieve the
desired results. Watch for a little deceit and use sensible everyday
precautions.

Card 4. The Star
When everything seems to have been lost, both externally and
internally, the guiding star appears. It points to a recovery, followed
by a renewal of faith for a brighter future.

Card 5. Ace of Cups
There is enormous potential for a very healthy relationship. With
care and consideration, this could develop into something much
deeper and more significant.

Card 6. The Fool
Start this fresh chapter of life with optimism. Use the knowledge and
experiences from the past to make this a positive new period.

Card 7. King of Cups
Healing, health and related professions are in focus. This potential
could be developed. The person however should give more attention
to his or her own needs.

Card 8. 4 of Cups
Relationship issues are less than satisfactory or non existent. A significant effort is required to improve the situation.

Card 9. 6 of Swords
A calm period is ahead where problems can be put aside. It is up to the individual concerned to be positive and resist the self-inflicted headaches of the past.

Card 10. 4 of Wands
The honesty, effort and shared commitment to a team or partnership pays dividends. It brings a well earned reward for both the personal and or professional relationship.

Card 11. 7 of Wands
This character needs action and must avoid stagnation. A fresh challenge should be found and new plans formulated.

Card 12. Queen of Cups
Someone who is deep emotionally and often intuitive. She may have been a victim in the past and now chooses to remain one. It is preferable though to make some positive changes.

Card 13. Page of Wands
Good news is here, which may have been awaited for some time. It is now possible to proceed with longer term plans.

Card 14. The Hermit
Time is precious. Clear out deep seated burdens from the past as they seriously limit the present. Only then is it possible for the real self to emerge.

Card 15. The Lovers
This complex and tempting personal situation requires careful consideration. Listen to and act on the inner voice of truth.

Comment
Although the time suggested is 6 months, it often takes longer to resolve the issues raised. It is clear from the appearance of The Fool, that this reading welcomes a whole new and positive long term section of the person's life. Supporting this, are the very positive cards from the action packed suit of wands. These include a significant person, of similar values and energy. It mirrors too, the client at her energetic, cheerful, leadership best.
Advice from the card of The Hermit needs to be resolved, in order for the enquirer to move forward confidently, open to a relationship worthy of her, as indicated by The Lovers. It remains as always with The Tarot, very much up to her. We wish her joy.

The Celtic Cross

This is used as a traditional spread to seek ideas on which to reflect, concerning a specific topic. It may vary slightly, between a 10 or 11 card layout

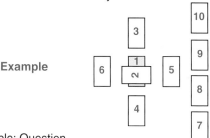

Example

Example: Question
Is there potential in a new friendship for something deeper, given that we both have past hurts?

Explanation of the position of each card.

Interpretation
1. The Magician. *Current conditions.* All these personal resources are here to be used. Keep a healthy, balanced and positive approach in this new era.

2. The Tower. *Associated hopes or problems.* A false exterior built protects or hides the truth. Now shattering events seem likely. Time is the healer. The new foundation will then be stronger, firmer and more authentic.

3. 2 of Cups. *Conscious wishes.* These two people are well matched, to further explore their goals and values. The focus is on the development of the harmony and trust already evident.

4. Temperance. *Subconscious wishes.* Things appear to be quite stagnant. With patience, promising new personal goals will soon appear on the horizon.

5. The Sun. *Influences behind the current situation.* True happiness is fully appreciated, as it has been fully earned. The real pleasures and joys of living are warmly shared.

6. 6 of Pentacles. *Immediate conditions in the short term.* This person knows that something more valuable than money makes life truly worthwhile. The goodness of kind deeds brings its own rewards.

7. 8 of cups. *Personal approach required.* At last the emotional upheavals of the past are left behind. Calm times lie ahead both personally and in relationships.

8. 4 of swords. *Factors along the way.* Quiet thought or prayer is needed, to cope with the daily demands of life. Here is a definite on-going responsibility to look after oneself, properly and regularly.

9. 10 of swords. *Fears related to the outcome if any.* May relate to the positive or negative approach of the enquirer. It is time to acknowledge the nightmare from the past. Only then is it possible to move on fully to welcome the new future.

10. 4 of wands. *Suggests the final outcome.* The honesty, effort and shared commitment to a team or partnership pays dividends. It brings a well earned reward for both the personal and or professional relationship.

Comment
The 3 major arcana cards set the scene and indicate the importance of the question, in terms of personal growth for the enquirer. The Magician confirms the readiness for the new, long term stage and The Tower acknowledges past barriers, put up to protect the inner self. The 10 of wands advises both people should relinquish the anguish of the past, as positive potential is waiting to be explored. The difficult times are behind them and it is now up to this couple to look after themselves as individuals, as shown in the 4 of swords. They should explore together the potential in their shared values of kindliness, financial balance and harmony. Will they follow the Tarot guidance?

Three Card Spread

This can be useful in putting things quickly into perspective. Lacking depth however, it should be used only occasionally. It is most useful for beginners learning to read the cards and practice their skills.

1. Think quietly of a question and concentrate on it as you start to shuffle the cards.
2. Shuffle the cards well and cut two or three times as usual.
3. Turn over the top 3 cards and set out from left to right.

Past Present Future
Example: Question
Is it timely to change the pace and direction of my employment ?

Past - The Empress

Present - Temperance

Future - 8 of Pentacles

| 1 | 2 | 3 |
| Past | Present | Future |

Past The focus is on a nurturing, nesting period. It is important though to retain the vital sense of personal identity.
Present Things appear to be quite stagnant. With patience, promising new personal goals will soon appear on the horizon.
Future A special talent should be used to develop in a new and personally satisfying direction. This may involve some long term changes, with renewed pleasure and profit in work.

Comment
It is clear that it is almost time to change pace and direction, exactly as the question suggested. The past has been kind to you. Enjoy the future.

Further Reading

The Tarot: Richard Cavendish :Michael Joseph : London : 1975.

The Tarot: Mouni Sadhu : Unwin Paperbacks : 1990 (Orig. G. Allen & Unwin Ltd. 1962)

The Enchanted Tarot: Amy Zerner & Monte Faber : St. Martin's Press ; New York.

The Mythical Tarot: Juliette Sharman Burke and Liz Greene: Simon and Schuster

Welcome
the journey

The Journey of a Thousand Miles Begins with a First Step...

the First Steps
series

·First Steps to Meditation

·First Steps to Massage

·First Steps to Tarot

·First Steps to Chi Kung

·First Steps to Dream Power

·First Steps to Yoga

Further titles following shortly:

·First Steps to Reflexology

·First Steps to Feng Shui

·First Steps to Managing Stress

·First Steps to Astrology

·First Steps to Chinese Herbal Medicine

·First Steps to Acupressure

First Steps to...

•AXIOM PUBLISHING
Unit 2, 1 Union Street, Stepney, South Australia, 5069